SPHE: 2nd Year

Minding Me 2
My Well-Being

Includes the SIX official Well-Being indicators

Social, Personal and Health Education

Fiona Chambers   Anne Jones   Anita Stackpoole

MENTOR

MENTOR BOOKS

43 Furze Road

Sandyford Industrial Estate

Dublin 18

Tel: 01-2952112

Fax: 01-2952114

Website: www.mentorbooks.ie

Email: admin@mentorbooks.ie

Text:	Fiona Chambers
	Anne Jones
	Anita Stackpoole
Subject editor:	Joan Rath
Edited by:	Emma Dunne
Artwork:	QBS Learning
Design and layout:	Kathryn O'Sullivan
Cover Design:	Kathryn O'Sullivan

Acknowledgements

The publisher would like to thank the following for permission to reproduce material: Carol Todd, Future Voices Ireland, HSE Sexual Health and Crisis Pregnancy Programme, Rory O'Neill, thejournal.ie.

The publisher has made every effort to trace and acknowledge the holders of copyright for material in this book. In the event of any copyright holder having been omitted, the publishers will come to a suitable arrangement at the first opportunity.

ISBN: 978-1-909417-64-9

Contents

Introduction

In the *Minding Me: My Well-Being* series, we want to create a space for you to stop and think about your well-being. You will learn about the steps you can take to ensure that you are happy, healthy and well. There are 8 key skills to help you feel your best and ready for life's challenges:

- being creative
- being literate (i.e. able to read, write and spell at the right level for your age-group)
- being numerate (i.e. able to understand mathematical reasoning and problem solve at the right level for your age-group)
- communicating
- managing information and thinking
- managing yourself
- staying well
- working with others

In this book, you will complete a number of activities that we have carefully designed to help you to develop these core life skills.

WB1	**Mental and emotional well-being** ● Clear thinking processes ● Recognising and expressing thoughts and feelings ● Responding positively
WB2	**Social well-being** ● Family relationships, friendships and other social relationships ● Feelings of belonging, compassion and caring ● Social support
WB3	**Physical well-being** ● The physical body – its growth, development and ability to move ● Ways of caring for your body
WB4	**Spiritual well-being** ● The values and beliefs that shape the way people live ● The search for meaning and purpose in life ● Personal identity and self-awareness (for some people and communities, spiritual well-being is linked to a particular religion; for others, it is not)

While moving through this book, the icons above will be helpful in identifying which type of well-being is being explored. All four types of well-being work together to ensure an overall sense of well-being.

We have also included the six official Well-being indicators. These six indicators appear regularly throughout the series:

The icons below are used to show you how SPHE links to other topics and skills.

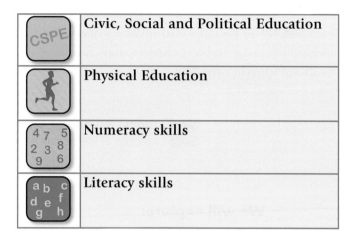

CSPE	**Civic, Social and Political Education**
	Physical Education
	Numeracy skills
	Literacy skills

Minding Me 2: My Well-Being will give you the opportunity to practise and build on the skills and knowledge you gained in First Year. As you move from First Year to Second Year, your sense of belonging will probably be greater. However *Minding Me 2: My Well-Being* will be very useful for you as you prepare for assignments and exams or make new friends and join different groups. This time can be challenging but also very exciting as you continue to learn more about yourself and others.

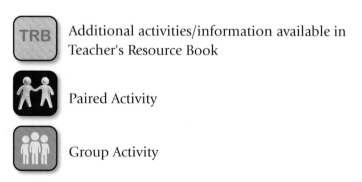

TRB	Additional activities/information available in Teacher's Resource Book
	Paired Activity
	Group Activity

Fiona, Anne and Anita

Module 1
Belonging and Integrating

In this module we will set the scene for an exciting year ahead. Being in Second Year brings new challenges, e.g. subject choices, new hobbies, new friends or new ways of working together in class.

 Digital Resources are available for this module at mentorbooks.ie/resources

We will explore:

1. Looking back, looking forward

Meeting up again after the summer holidays can certainly add to that 'back to business' buzz in the classroom. The most important business in most students' minds will be finding out what their classmates were up to over the summer.

Paired
ACTIVITY

1 **My summer**

(a) Answer the questions below to help remind you of summer events you might wish to share with a partner.

(i) How would you describe your summer (active, quiet, etc.)?

_____

_____

(ii) What was the highlight of your summer – your best experience?

_____

_____

(iii) Did you achieve something of which you are especially proud?

_____

_____

(b) Now with your partner, take turns to read your answers to one another.

2 **Remembering First Year**

As you moved through First Year, you gathered many memories ...

(a) On each rung of the ladder, write down a key memory from First Year (include at least one positive memory and one negative memory).

‘Pleasure is the flower that passes; Remembrance, the lasting perfume.’

Jean de Boufflers, French writer

(b) Looking at the ladder, highlight your favourite memory of First Year. Describe this memory here and say why it is so important to you.

_____

_____

_____

_____

(c) Looking at the ladder, highlight your least favourite memory of First Year and explain why it was not a good experience for you.

_____

_____

_____

_____

(d) If you experienced this again, how might you deal with it now? Can you think of someone you could ask for help?

_____

_____

_____

WB4

1.

2.

3.

4.

5.

Personal goal-setting

Starting school again, but this time as a Second-Year student, can be seen as a fresh start. The new year is yours to make the best of. A simple way to make a good start is to set yourself goals. The goals can range from becoming more organised to being more patient or less stressed out. The goals you set must be your own.

5 **Setting personal goals**

(a) Looking at the headings for the footballs below, think of four goals you want to achieve during your second year in school. Write one of these goals in the space on each football. The last football is blank for a goal of your choice.

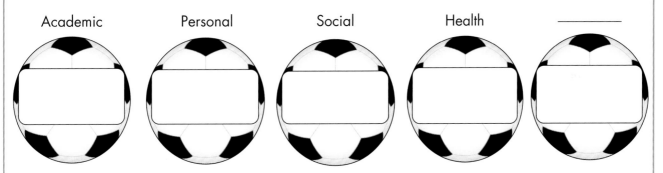

Academic   Personal   Social   Health   _____

(b) Now fill in the table below, describing the steps you will take and how long you will give yourself to achieve each goal listed in the footballs above.

Goal	Steps to achieve goal	How long to achieve goal
Academic		
Personal		
Social		
Health		
_____		

ACTIVITY

WB1

WB2

6 **Setting group goals**

A logo is a design or symbol that identifies an organisation. It can use text, e.g. Coca-Cola, an image, e.g. the Nike Swoosh, or a combination of these.

(a) In just one minute, create your own personal logo. The purpose of your logo is to create a memorable image to represent you. The image you present of yourself could show the values or emotions that you think are important. The following ideas may help you to do this:
(i) Include your initials.
(ii) Include an image or images of things you like/like to do.
(iii) Try and include a hidden meaning – for example, the Nike logo represents the wings of the Greek goddess of victory, Nike, and is meant to suggest movement.

Show your logo to your partner and explain its meaning.

(b) Now divide into groups of three to six. The group goal is for each group to design a logo in 10 minutes that represents them as a team. Each group must appoint a leader to share with the class the ideas that led to the team's logos and what the logos say about them.

(c) As a class, discuss the following sentences and write the agreed answers in the spaces below.
(i) The personal benefits of goal setting are

_____

_____

(ii) The steps we used in our goal-setting process were

_____

_____

(iii) Group goal setting boosts everyone's self-confidence by

_____

_____

TRB

2. Group work

WB1   WB2

When it comes to problem solving, the old saying 'two heads are better than one' certainly makes sense. Teamwork/group work has many positives.

Teams can be more successful and motivated than individuals trying to solve problems on their own.

Working in teams can help a group find a solution to a problem in a social, safe and supportive way (cooperative learning).

Working on group projects, such as Tidy Towns, can help students develop valuable skills that are sought after in the professional world today, such as leadership and motivating others.

Positive group experiences, where all participants share equally and are open to ideas, can add to student learning and help students to remember important information.

Fire ants know how to survive when the waters rise. They turn their bodies into life rafts through teamwork. Linked together, the ants can form a watertight seal that keeps the group from drowning. As a whole, the fire ants' rafts are significantly more buoyant than an individual fire ant floating alone.

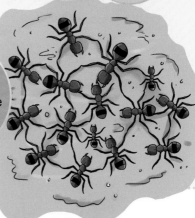

Group ACTIVITY

TRB

1. **Working in teams**

   In groups, discuss the following:

   (a) What do you think teamwork is?
   (b) What do you think the benefits of teamwork are to
   ● The individual
   ● The team

2. **Class charter**

   From the experience you have of working in groups in SPHE last year, design a new class charter for group work using the following guidelines.

   (a) Decide five ground rules and rank them 1–5 with 1 being the most important.
   (b) Share these rules with the class and decide which rules to include in the class charter for group work on page 14.

CSPE

✂ **Remember!**

These rules must protect the rights of everyone in your group.
Everyone has **rights** but they also have **responsibilities**.

What do you think ...?

A right is
_____
_____
_____
Example: the right to education

A responsibility is
_____
_____
_____
Example: the responsibility to learn as well as you can

WB4

Class charter for group work

1. _____

2. _____

3. _____

4. _____

5. _____

Signed:
_____

Date:
_____

3. Family ties

Changes in modern families

While the idea of who makes up a family has changed over the years, family still continues to be central to our lives.

In recent times, the traditional 'nuclear family' has grown to include many different relationships. Modern families are more diverse now with many different lifestyles and living arrangements. Some families have a large network of in-laws, half-siblings (sisters and brothers), foster sisters and brothers and partners. In your school and in your life, you will meet people from a range of family backgrounds.

Different kinds of families

The days of judging someone based on their family background are in the past. We have a responsibility to respect difference, including the different arrangements of modern families, and ensure everyone has equal opportunities to reach their full potential.

John Lennon of the Beatles was raised by his aunt from three years of age. Steve Jobs, the genius behind Apple computers, was adopted as a child. 50 Cent, the hip-hop mogul, was adopted by his grandmother.

❝ Variety's the very spice of life
that gives it all its flavour. ❞

William Cowper, poet

❝ Family isn't always blood. It's the people in your life
who want you in theirs; the ones who accept you for
who you are. The ones who would do anything to
see you smile and who love you no matter what. ❞

www.spirituallythinking.blogspot.com

ACTIVITY

1 **Family tree**

Over the past year you have changed on many levels: physically, emotionally, socially and, perhaps, spiritually.

WB1

WB2

WB4

(a) Write your name on the trunk of the tree below. Then on the branches write in the names of all your family members. Their position on the tree indicates how close or distant you feel to them.

(b) Who are you closest to in your family?

_____

(i) Why do you think that is?

_____

(ii) Have you always been close to this person?

_____

(c) Who is most distant on the tree?

_____

(i) What are the reasons for this?

_____

(ii) Is there anything you might do to change this?

_____

(d) Who do you respect most?

_____

(i) Why?

_____

(ii) Has this person always been a role model for you?

_____

You may have noticed that your relationships with family members change as you grow and develop. This is because you are forming values and learning about what is important for you. You are developing opinions on the world around you. Some people will naturally be closer to us than others and this can change with different experiences. This is a normal part of our relationships with others.

End of Module Review

WB1

Sometimes it is the little things that a person does for someone else that say a lot about how much they care for them. In the space below describe a time when someone said or did something small for you that made you feel valued and special.

_____

_____

_____

_____

_____

_____

_____

_____

_____

_____

_____

_____

_____

Module 2
Self-Management

In Module 1 you set goals for your new school year. This module will help you to achieve those goals.

 Digital Resources are available for this module at mentorbooks.ie/resources

We will explore:

1 Motivation 19

2 Study skills 26

1. Motivation

Motivation is the reason or reasons we have for acting or behaving in a particular way. It is the general desire or willingness of someone to do something.

ACTIVITY

1 **What motivates me?**

(a) Fill in the boxes below with words or pictures.

Three things I'd like to have	Three things I'd like to do	What I'd like to be doing in 10 years' time

(b) What or who has motivated you to want, or want to do, these things?

_____

_____

(c) Do you think these things will be good for you? Why?

_____

_____

In order to decide whether something is good for us or not, we need to have a very strong sense of self-worth or self-esteem. In other words, we need to believe in ourselves. If we have a strong sense of self-esteem, we will be motivated in a positive way.

Self-esteem and self-confidence

- Self-esteem is the value or worth we place on ourselves. We create this image of ourselves from how family and friends act around us.
- Some people have low self-esteem and this is often due to negative/bad comments or experiences, e.g. being bullied.
- People have positive or high self-esteem when they feel good about themselves and the people around them. Nobody has high self-esteem all the time, but your worth as a person never changes.

Self-confidence

- If someone has high self-esteem they will also have self-confidence.
- Self-confidence is how we think of ourselves in certain situations and how other people react to us, e.g. 'Jimmy is good at French and weak at Maths.' So Jimmy will probably have more confidence in French class than Maths class.

How to build self-confidence

To build up our confidence we should
- Know which things we can do well
- Work well with others
- Know our responsibilities
- Accept our limitations

2 **What does confident behaviour look like?**

(a) Look at the list of behaviours in the table below. For each behaviour, tick whether you associate it with high self-confidence or low self-confidence.

WB2

Behaviour		High	Low
(i)	Behaving in a way you think other people want you to		
(ii)	Staying in your comfort zone		
(iii)	Doing what you believe is right		
(iv)	Dismissing compliments about your achievements		
(v)	Admitting you made a mistake and learning from it		
(vi)	Covering up mistakes and hoping no one notices		
(vii)	Being willing to take a risk		
(viii)	Accepting compliments politely		

(b) Discuss with your partner your reasons for your choices.

Building self-confidence

WB2

Building self-confidence is achievable for everyone. It takes planning and time but it's well worth the effort.

Ways to build self-confidence

1. Look at what you have achieved to date. Throughout our daily lives we achieve many small things, e.g. completing the day's homework. Likewise we also have bigger achievements in our lives, e.g. getting on the hurling or camogie team, learning to swim, making a new friend, improving reading ability, representing the school. All these achievements, however big or small, help to build our self-confidence.

2. What are you good at? It's important to remember that everybody is good at something. For some people it can be schoolwork, for others it can be sports, for others it can be art or music etc. Knowing what your strengths are is important to help with your feelings of self-confidence.

3. Who are the important people and what are the important things in your life? Everyone has important people and things in their lives – it could be family, friends, neighbours or your bike, guitar etc.

4. What do you want to achieve? It is good for our self-confidence to know what we want to achieve. Setting goals, both long- and short-term, can help us feel better about ourselves.

5. Manage your mind – defeat negative self-talk. The only person who knows about your negative self-talk is you, so it's important to know how to counteract this by telling yourself the things that are good about you, e.g I'm a really kind friend; I am good at playing music; I love the colour of my eyes/hair etc.

ACTIVITY

3 **Building your own self-confidence**

Answer the following.

(a) Name something small you have achieved this week.

_____

(b) Name something big you have achieved since starting secondary school.

_____

(c) Name two things you are good at.

_____

(d) Name one important person and one important thing in your life.

_____

(e) Name one goal you would like to achieve this year.

_____

(f) Name one goal you would like to achieve by the end of secondary school.

_____

(g) Name two things that you like about yourself.

_____

_____

4 **My milestones**

Many years ago, stones were placed along roadsides to let a traveller know how many miles it was to the next town. These were known as milestones, marking important points along the journey, e.g. your first day at school, going to the shops on your own. We now use the term 'milestones' to describe important points along our journey through life.

Can you identify five key milestones in your life up to this point?

(a) _____

(b) _____

(c) _____

(d) _____

(e) _____

5 **The best day**

Imagine your best day possible and complete the following:

(a) I would be at

_____

(b) I would be doing

_____

(c) I would be with

_____

(d) I would be feeling

_____

Group ACTIVITY

6 **'Risking' by Patty Hansen**

Two seeds lay side by side in the fertile soil. The first seed said, 'I want to grow! I want to send my roots deep into the soil beneath me, and thrust my sprouts through the earth's crust above me. I want to unfurl my tender buds like banners to announce the arrival of spring. I want to feel the warmth of the sun on my face and the blessing of the morning dew on my petals!'

And so she grew.

The second seed said, 'I am afraid. If I send my roots into the ground below, I don't know what I will encounter in the dark. If I push my way through the hard soil above me I may damage my delicate sprouts. What if I let my buds open and a snail tries to eat them? And if I were to open my blossoms, a small child may pull me from the ground. No, it is much better for me to wait until it is safe.'

And so she waited.

A yard hen scratching around in the early spring ground for food found the waiting seed and promptly ate it.

The moral of the story: Those of us who find it hard to risk and grow may get swallowed up by life.

As a class, discuss the following questions.

(a) How did the first seed show self-confidence?

(b) How did the second seed show lack of self-esteem?

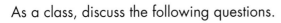

7 My declaration of self-esteem

I am me. In all the world there is no one else exactly like me. Everything that comes out of me is authentically (genuinely) mine because I alone chose it. I own everything about me: my body, my feelings, my mouth, my voice, all my actions, whether they be to others or to myself. I own my fantasies, my dreams, my hopes, my fears. I own my triumphs and successes, all my failures and mistakes. Because I own all of me, I can become intimately acquainted with me. By so doing, I can love me and be friendly with all my parts. I know there are aspects about myself that puzzle me and other aspects that I do not know, but as long as I am friendly and loving to myself, I can courageously and hopefully look for solutions to the puzzles and ways to find out more about me. However I look and sound, whatever I say and do, and whatever I think and feel at a given moment in time is authentically me. If, later, some parts of how I looked, sounded, thought and felt turn out to be unfitting, I can discard that which is unfitting, keep the rest and invent something new for that which I discarded. I can see, hear, feel, think, say and do. I have the tools to survive, to be close to others, to be productive, and to make sense and order out of the world of people and things outside of me. I own me, and therefore, I can engineer me. I am me and I am okay.

How do you feel having read this? Take a moment to think about it.

_____

_____

8 The 'I am' percentage poem

(a) Look at the poem below and then write your own poem about yourself.

I'm 30% loveable

I'm 30% kind

I'm 20% musical

I'm 20% sporty

(b) Now represent the information in your poem on a pie chart.

9 **Advice**

Your best friend has had very little confidence since they were bullied in First Year, and you would like to help them.

What are the five pieces of advice you would give them?

(a) _____

(b) _____

(c) _____

(d) _____

(e) _____

‘ *Believe in yourself and you can do unbelievable things.* ’

Unknown

10 **My self-esteem today**

I like myself because _____

I feel good about _____

I laugh when I think about_____

I get excited about _____

My favourite place is _____

My friends say I am good at_____

I consider myself a good _____

The person I admire the most is _____

My goal for the future is_____

2. Study skills

As you progress through school and on to further education, knowing how *you* study and what method works best for you is an important skill to have.

At the moment you may be studying towards a class exam, and you may have an assignment or project to complete. Each of these will require you to plan and build time into your week for them.

Creating a timetable of your week is very useful as it helps you to know when assignments and homework are due. Putting reminders in your phone is also helpful.

① **Getting organised**

Fill in the weekly timetable below, including information about homework, assignments, other activities, meeting friends etc.

Monday			
Tuesday			
Wednesday			
Thursday			
Friday			
Saturday			
Sunday			

Study habits – quick reference guide

1. Spread out your study sessions over the week.
2. Study at the same time every day.
3. Start to study when you planned to.
4. Set specific goals for each study session.
5. Start with your most challenging piece of work.

2 List four reasons why you study or do your homework.

(a) _____

(b) _____

(c) _____

(d) _____

The How? Where? When? What? of study

How?

Remember everyone will have a different way of organising their study time.

1. Be organised.
2. Plan ahead: know what subjects you are going to study and have the books and notes that you need for this subject to hand.
3. Make written notes as you study – have a different copy or notebook for each subject.
4. Present your work clearly and neatly.
5. List possible questions in your revision notebooks to help you prepare for exams.
6. Ask someone at home to examine you on the information you have learned.

Where?

1. Study in a quiet place with no distractions.
2. Turn off your mobile phone, music and TV. Have good lighting, heating and ventilation.
3. Try to create the same atmosphere as an exam centre.

When?

1. Each school day will require study and homework time.
2. Time will have to be set aside for study at the weekend as well.
3. Pick a day that suits you.
4. Try to study at the same time every day.
5. During exam time, e.g. Christmas, summer, Junior Cycle, you may have less time for other activities until the exam is over.
6. Look forward to your holidays and the break from school and homework.

What?

1. Check your journal or homework notebook.
2. Divide your time between learning and written homework.
3. Use a time plan to decide which subjects you need to study.
4. Use questions in your textbook to help you with your learning.
5. Make notes by putting the information into your own words.
6. If you don't understand something, ask your teacher the next day in class.

 Remember!

Everybody will have different study methods, so find out what works best for you.

Understanding terms

When we don't understand a question, it is difficult to answer. Becoming familiar with the key words used in exam questions will help you in your answers. Below is a list of words and phrases that regularly appear in exam questions.

Word/phrase	Explanation
Enumerate/List/State	List the points; no detailed explanation is necessary.
Characteristics	List the qualities.
Principle	Give a reason or a description of a working method.
Properties	List the features of a substance, e.g. fat, soluble, etc.
Define	Write down the precise meaning of a word or phrase. In some cases it may be necessary to give an example or a very brief description.
Select/Name/Suggest	State the answer in one or two words. There is no need for detail.
Outline	Write one or two sentences on each point, i.e. give a brief description.
Describe	Give a written description in point form. Use a diagram to back up your answer if possible.
Explain	Give a detailed account, back up your answer with a specific example and include a diagram if applicable.
Discuss/Give an account of	This requires a very detailed description of what is being asked. Remember to structure your answer in point form. Provide at least six points in your answer.
Informative paragraph	Provide at least five points in your answer and structure it in point form.
Classify	Group the items into categories.
Evaluate	Make an assessment of the worth of something; this could refer to negative and positive, uses, etc.
Illustrate	Make something clear by the use of concrete examples (diagrams) to explain or clarify a point.

TRB

List three study tips that you've learned from this module that you will incorporate into your own study routine.

(a) _____

(b) _____

(c) _____

Module 3
Communication Skills

When we give or receive messages we are communicating with others. In Module 3 of *Minding Me 1: My Well-Being*, we learned that these messages can be spoken, written or shown through our body language. We discovered the importance of expressing ourselves clearly through what we say, what we write and how we behave. Learning to communicate in a positive way with those around us is a very important skill for a happy and healthy life. This module aims to improve your communication skills with the people around you.

 Digital Resources are available for this module at mentorbooks.ie/resources

We will explore:

1 **Assertive communication** 31

2 **Communication breakdown** 34

1. Assertive communication

> *Sticking up for yourself means knowing who you are and what you stand for, and being true to yourself*
>
> *Kaufman, Raphael and Espeland, 'Stick up for Yourself'.*

Assertiveness is a healthy way of communicating. It enables us to speak up for ourselves directly, truthfully and respectfully. Every day, you will find yourself in situations where being assertive can help – like asking a group of classmates if you can join them for lunch, approaching a teacher with a question or returning a faulty purchase to a shop. Sometimes people confuse being assertive with being aggressive. However, assertiveness is neither aggressive nor passive. It lies in the middle.

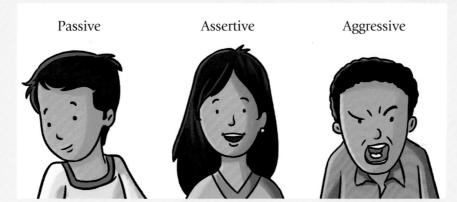

Passive   Assertive   Aggressive

What it means to be assertive:

- You can give an opinion or say how you feel.
- You can ask for what you want or need.
- You can disagree respectfully.
- You can offer your ideas and suggestions calmly and clearly.
- You can say no without feeling guilty.
- You can speak up for someone else.
- You keep good eye contact in conversations.

(Assertiveness, www.kidshealth.org)

Why does being assertive matter?

Being assertive matters because *you* matter – it shows that you believe in yourself and are confident of your place in the world. It can give you the strength to deal with conflict and to stand up for yourself and others.

Being assertive is essential for success in all areas of life, including politics and movie-making.

(1) **Body language**

(a) List three features of a passive person's body language.

(i) _____

(ii) _____

(iii) _____

(b) List three features of an assertive person's body language.

(i) _____

(ii) _____

(iii) _____

Sometimes we can feel a bit shy. To help us to become more assertive, we might first need to overcome shyness.

Three steps to overcome shyness

1. **Try chatting to people who know you very well:** It may be easier to practise eye contact, smiling, confident body language and starting up a conversation with family and friends. When you feel confident you can branch out to people that you know less well, e.g. your teacher, a local shopkeeper etc.

2. **Think of ways to begin a conversation:** It's often a good idea to have a few ideas ready beforehand, e.g. 'That colour is nice on you!' 'Did you see the match last night?' 'What homework do we have for Maths tonight?'

3. **Practise your conversation:** Sometimes we avoid a conversation because we are feeling shy. It is a really good idea to write down what you want to say in a conversation so that you are clear and prepared before you start.

To communicate assertively:

- Use a clear, firm, calm voice.
- Look the person in the eye with a confident expression.
- Keep your head up and shoulders back in a confident posture.

NOTE
Watch Amy Cuddy's TED Talk 'Your body language shapes who you are' (www.ted.com). Fake it till you make it!

Understanding other people's perspectives

WB2

In Module 3 of *Minding Me 1: My Well-Being*, we learned that communication was a form of code. Basically, when you speak or write or draw, you are making up a code for others to interpret. You are also trying to understand the codes of those around you. In this module, we want to try to understand the perspectives (points of view) of others. This is done by listening to what a person says and by watching their body language. By doing this, we can learn to be more assertive.

ACTIVITY

(2) **How to be assertive in different situations**

Listed below are four situations where you need to be assertive. Draw a comic strip with speech bubbles to show how you would handle each situation assertively.

Shop assistant: **You are returning a set of earphones that won't work.**

Teacher: **You are asking permission to go to a match during class time.**

Parent: **You are asking to go to a disco.**

Friend: **You are explaining that you don't want to meet up.**

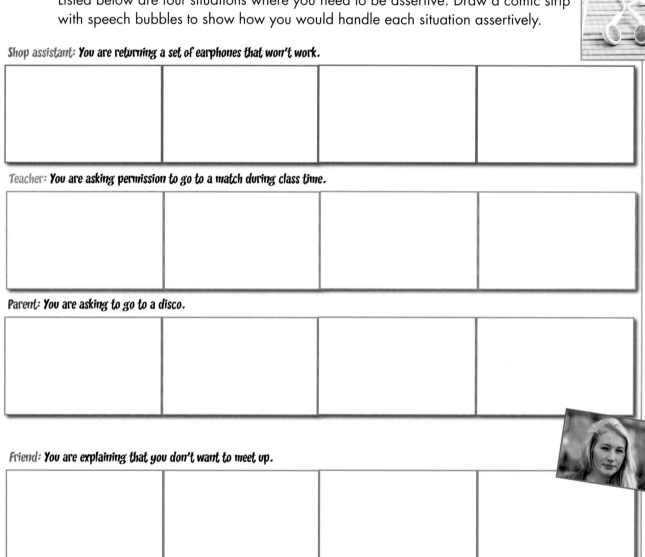

2. Communication breakdown

Even when you try to be mannerly and behave correctly when communicating your message, communication can still break down. There are a number of reasons why this might happen.

(i)   **Language:** the same word may mean different things to different people.
(ii) **Too much information:** if too much information is given, the person might not have time to take it all in.

(iii) **Not paying attention:** the person we are communicating with might not be fully listening to us or reading our email/text properly.

(iv) **Distraction/noise:** trying to communicate in a noisy place with poor lighting etc. can change the message.

(v) **Emotions:** how the person receives the message will depend on their mood at the time. If they are not in a good mood, they may react badly to your message.

(vi) **Forgetfulness:** sometimes people can forget what you have told them or emailed them.

TRB

Group ACTIVITY

1. **Reasons for communication breakdown**

(a) With your partner look at the reasons listed on page 34 and above and try to find an example of each reason for communication breakdown.

(i) _____

(ii) _____

(iii) _____

(iv) _____

(v) _____

(vi) _____

(b) Having studied the list above, break into small groups and find six ways in which you think communication breakdown could be avoided.

 **Remember!**

Also keep in mind communication etiquette and netiquette from pages 36 and 37, Module 3: Communication Skills, *Minding Me 1: My Well-Being.*

NOTE

Etiquette is being mannerly and behaving in the correct way with people. When we communicate, we always try to be mannerly and to behave well. This is communication etiquette.

NOTE

Netiquette is the name given to the manners and behaviour we should show when we are online.

End of Module Review

You receive the text on the right from your friend in the middle of the night and it wakes you up.

(a) Consider how an **aggressive** person, a **passive** person and an **assertive** person might respond to this text. Write their responses in the relevant phone screens below.

> Hey. Bring ur blue dress to school tomoz. Need it for disco Sat. Don't forget …

Aggressive

Passive

Assertive

(b) How can you avoid communication breakdown with this friend?

_____

_____

_____

_____

Module 4
Physical Health

Physical health is very important for our overall well-being. It's essential to learn about how to take care of our bodies, whether we are feeling our best or feeling unwell.

 Digital Resources are available for this module at mentorbooks.ie/resources

We will explore:

1. Body care

 Remember!

When we look good, we feel good. Feeling good enhances our self-esteem.

NOTE
Hygiene is another word for cleanliness.

TRB

 **ACTIVITY**

1. **How do you stay clean every day?**

   (a) In the table below can you list the body-care routines you carry out every day?

Routine	Why I do this

   (b) Circle any routines that you have only started doing since starting secondary school.

2. **Finding the right information**

   (a) Where do you think you would find information on how to be more hygienic?

   _____

   _____

   _____

   (b) Why is it important to get the right information on staying clean?

   _____

   _____

   _____

Group ACTIVITY

3 **Skin**

In small groups, discuss the following questions.

(a) What basic hygiene rules should you follow to ensure you have clean skin?

(b) Can you think of any skin problems teenagers might have?

(c) Why do you think that teenagers in particular tend to have skin problems? What causes them?

NOTE
See MM1: My Well Being, Module 4, page 55

Hair care

Hair facts

● Every month hair grows about 1 cm.

● Each person has about 100,000 hairs on their head.

● Every day you lose 100 hairs.

● Brushing your hair is important as it stimulates the scalp and helps remove dirt.

● Greasy hair is caused by an over-production of oil from the scalp.

● Split ends can occur as a result of using a brush on wet hair. Overuse of hairdryers, hair straighteners and hair dye can also cause split ends. Having your hair cut regularly reduces the appearance of split ends.

● How often you need to wash your hair depends on the type of hair you have. Hair prone to being greasy will need frequent washing, while dry hair will need less.

Paired ACTIVITY

4 **Healthy hair**

With your partner, make a list of five guidelines to follow in order to have healthy hair.

(a) _____

(b) _____

(c) _____

(d) _____

(e) _____

Hair problems

1. **Dandruff:** this is an extremely common problem that occurs when the scalp sheds its skin in large flakes rather than as a fine dust.

   The larger flakes are visible on the hair and on clothing.

   To treat it, use a specially medicated anti-dandruff shampoo or, if it still doesn't clear up, visit your doctor who can give you a prescription shampoo.

2. **Head lice:** these tiny insects like to live in your hair. They multiply extremely quickly and then attach themselves to your hair.

   They produce eggs called nits, which cling to your hair as well.

   Lice can be picked up very easily in a crowded place, e.g. school.

   If you notice lice, treat your hair immediately with special lotion from the chemist.

Feet

- Our feet carry us around from the moment we can walk.
- Did you know that during your lifetime you are likely to walk 115,000 miles!
- People develop foot problems due to ill-fitting shoes, injury, wear and tear or as part of a disease (e.g. diabetes).
- Chiropodists are medical professionals who specialise in treating foot problems.
- Shoes soak up sweat and therefore need time to dry out.
- Try to have two pairs of shoes so you can alternate between pairs.

Things that can grow on our feet!

- **Athlete's foot:** this is a fungus that grows between your toes.
- **Bunions:** wearing shoes that are too narrow can cause swelling of the joints in the big toe.
- **Corns:** these are areas of hard skin with a root in the middle that occur when shoes don't fit properly.
- **Ingrowing toenails:** these occur if you cut your nails in the wrong shape (remember to cut straight across) or if you wear shoes that are too narrow.
- **Verrucae:** these are painful, irritating warts that develop on the soles of your feet.

Feet rules

- Never wear anyone else's shoes.
- Wash your feet daily and dry them thoroughly.
- Cut your toenails regularly, straight across.
- Buy shoes that fit you properly.
- Change your socks (and/or tights) daily.
- Never walk barefoot around a swimming pool.

☞ ✂ **Remember!**

Your foot care should be preventative and something you do throughout your life.

ACTIVITY

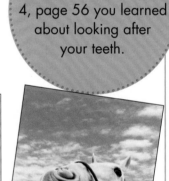
NOTE
In *Minding Me 1: My Well Being*, Module 4, page 56 you learned about looking after your teeth.

(5) Teeth

In the space below, describe how you take care of your teeth on a daily basis.

Body image

When we look after our bodies correctly we show respect for ourselves. This can help form a positive body image. Sometimes people have difficulty identifying the positive sides of themselves, especially in relation to their bodies. It is important to respect and appreciate your body the way it is. You can show this by the way you treat it.

6 **Positive body image**

What do you think the link is between personal hygiene and a positive body image?

_____

_____

Hygiene in the home

'The connection between health and the dwelling (the home) of the population is one of the most important that exists.'

Florence Nightingale

Research has shown that indoor air can be up to five times more polluted than the outdoors. The person in an unclean home is breathing in dust mites, pet dander, pollen, mould, bug skeletons and toxins from cleaning products. Many symptoms, such as itchy eyes, runny nose and wheezing, which are usually attributed to allergies, could instead be caused by an unclean house.

(7) **What lurks in your bedroom?**

Keeping your environment clean and tidy can help keep your body healthy. Picture your bedroom. How did you leave it this morning? Look at the list in the table below and indicate which items apply to your room. Then write in what effect you think that item might have on your health.

	Yes	No	Effect on health
Unmade bed?			
Unchanged bedclothes?			
Food?			
Glasses of water?			
Dirty tissues?			
Dirty laundry?			

2. Feeling unwell

Throughout our lives there will be times when we feel unwell. Sometimes we just need to stay at home for a couple of days and rest, while other times we need to get help from a professional. Different medical professionals specialise in certain ailments. Your GP may refer you to one of these specialists if they feel you need further help. Sometimes this can involve a visit to the relevant consultant or a stay in hospital. It is important to know when you need to seek outside advice.

(1) In the table opposite, write the type of medical professional who specialises in each body part listed.

Body Part	Professional
Eyes	
Teeth	
Feet	
Ears	
Back	

Visiting the doctor

When you visit the doctor, he or she is usually the one asking the questions. However, there are times when it might be appropriate for you to ask questions regarding medication or tests that you receive.

Here are some common questions that you might ask your doctor. Can you add to the list?

1. What causes this type of problem?
2. Is it serious?
3. Can I pass it on to other people? If so, how?
4. Is there anything I can do to help myself get better?
5. How can I prevent it from happening in the future?
6. What will this medicine do for me?
7. Will there be any side effects?
8. If yes, what are they?
9. How long will I need to take the medication for?
10. Is this test necessary?
11. Are there any risks involved?
12. Will this test or treatment hurt me?
13. Do I need to go to outpatients for this test?
14. _____
15. _____

TRB

Common illnesses and conditions in teenagers

As a teenager, and right throughout your life, you may suffer from or know someone who has experience of some of the following illnesses and conditions.

Acne

- Acne is a skin condition that is recognised by spots or pimples on the face, chest, neck and back.
- Acne can be mild, moderate or severe. It can sometimes lead to scarring and indentations on the skin.
- It is caused by one of the following: excess sebum production, bacterial infection or inflammation and hormonal changes.

How is acne treated?

Acne can be treated by oral prescriptive medicine or by a topical agent, e.g. cream or gel. Eating a healthy, balanced diet and drinking plenty of water can help reduce acne flare-ups.

Menstrual cramps (dysmenorrhoea)

- Between 30% and 60% of women suffer menstrual cramps every month. The severity of these can vary from individual to individual, depending on lifestyle, genetics and dietary choices.

- Cramps can consist of a sharp or dull pain in the pelvic region or lower back 2–3 days before the period begins. This is called PMT (pre-menstrual tension).

- Other common symptoms include backaches, headaches, pain in the inner thighs, diarrhoea or constipation, nausea and vomiting, dizziness, bloating, weight gain and breast tenderness.

- In some women and girls these symptoms can be severe and require further investigation by a doctor to determine why the pain is so bad or prolonged.

What is the best treatment?

- Having a warm, relaxing bath can relieve the pain. As a last resort, you could take some mild painkillers, but always check with your doctor first.

- Exercising on a regular basis, eating a balanced diet and reducing your intake of caffeine and salt (too much salt or caffeine can lead to water retention and add to a feeling of bloatedness) are all thought to ease the discomfort.

- Some people find that alternative forms of medicine are helpful in treating period pains, e.g. acupressure, acupuncture and various herbal remedies like evening primrose oil.

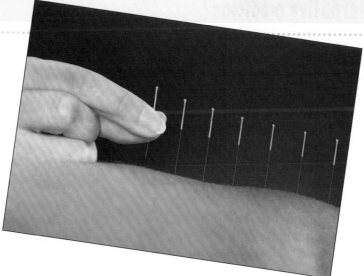

ACTIVITY

(2) **Common illnesses**

From the following list of common illnesses that teenagers may suffer from, list the symptoms and available treatments and say whether you should seek outside help or advice.

Illness/ailment	Symptoms	Treatment	Professional advice
Allergies			
Anaemia			
Asthma			
Cold sores			
Flu			
Headache			
Meningitis			
Migraine			

What is alternative medicine?

WB3

There are many types of alternative medicine available today, including traditional Chinese medicine (TCM), Ayurveda (the ancient Indian system of healing), homeopathy, naturopathy and osteopathy. Alternative medicine involves using natural remedies and treating the whole person as opposed to the specific area or symptom.

It is important to remember that there is no government legislation regarding these practices yet, although it is expected there will be in the near future.

End of Module Review

You might be familiar with the TAG process from your English classes. **TAG** stands for **Tell Ask Give**. In the table below, tell something you have learned from this module. Ask a question – is there anything else you would like to learn more about? And give a suggestion – offer a tip or some advice that wasn't mentioned in this module.

T	
A	
G	

Module 5
Friendship

Friendships are very important in our lives, but they can also change over time. In this module we will examine how this happens, and we will also look at bullying behaviour and its impacts.

 Digital Resources are available for this module at mentorbooks.ie/resources

We will explore:

1. The changing nature of friendship

The relationship between friends has to go through some change over time. This change does not always signal an end to the friendship. Once both friends are happy, agree on the need for change and are willing to make the change, both can grow and share the experience together. However, a friendship may end when new interests seem more attractive to one person than the other.

Paired ACTIVITY

1 **New opportunities in a new school**

With your partner, discuss the new opportunities that might arise in secondary school under the following headings:

(a) New friendships

(c) New subjects

(b) New class groups

(d) New teacher

Fading friendship

MOTHER: How was school today? You and Kirsty settling in OK?

LEAH: Yeah, it's going fine but I don't see Kirsty around so much.

MOTHER: Did you fall out with each other? We couldn't keep you apart in primary school!

LEAH: No, we haven't had a row. We just seem to have drifted apart. We talk to each other a little but not as much as we used to.

MOTHER: How do you feel about that?

LEAH: It's all right – we're in different classes now so I'm getting to know a lot more girls, especially in my art class.

MOTHER: That sounds good. I bet Kirsty is thriving in music. I wonder how her music teacher manages to stop her from singing!

Both laugh...

Life can take people in new directions. Growing apart from old friends is as natural as getting to know new people.

Paired ACTIVITY

(2) **Accepting change**

With your partner, suggest three ways to help accept the changing nature of friendship.

(a) _____

(b) _____

(c) _____

Friendship tips

1. **Accept what each person offers you as a friend:** One person might be a great listener, someone else a great advisor or a great laugh. Value that friend for the unique quality they share with you.

2. **Give only what you can.** Your friendship should not be based on people-pleasing, i.e. doing something only to make someone else happy. If you are feeling guilty for doing things that you really don't want to do, this may mean you are giving too much. A true friend should accept and understand your limits (see also Module 3: Communication skills). Learn to be assertive – true friends will really respect you for this.

3. **Hold onto great memories.** The good times you shared don't have to fade even if the friendship does. Think of your friend often, laugh about the fun times and share old stories. Moving on does not mean forgetting how you and your friend connected in the past. People come into our lives for particular reasons, but as life moves on things may change. Be thankful for all the special times with your friends.

What you would do for a friend

Being a good friend does not come with a handbook. Our personalities are unique and our life experiences are all different so that means there are many elements to consider when making a decision within a friendship. The bond between friends can be strong, but sometimes the power of this strength is held by only one person within the relationship to the disadvantage of the other. Knowing where to draw the line in a friendship is very important for self-protection and self-respect (see also Module 8: Influences and Decisions).

ACTIVITY

WB1

WB2

(3) **How should good friends behave?**

Read the statements below and answer the questions underneath each one.

(a) Lisa's friend Julie is losing interest in the things she used to enjoy. She says it's hard to take an interest in doing anything anymore and it's something no one could ever understand. Lisa wonders if she should tell Julie's mother about it.

    (i)   Should Lisa: speak up ☐   walk away ☐   tell someone ☐?

    (ii) Explain the reason for your answer.

    _____

    _____

(b) Clara is a great laugh – she is always doing daredevil stuff and gets away with it. Her latest trick is shoplifting. She takes clothes into the changing room, tries them on, then puts her own clothes on over them and leaves the shop. She needs her friend Lou to distract the security guards by behaving suspiciously. Clara says Lou won't get into any trouble.

    (i)   Should Lou: speak up ☐   walk away ☐   tell someone ☐?

    (ii) Explain the reason for your answer.

    _____

    _____

(c) Dan and Karl are good friends and go to the same school. Dan recently broke up with his girlfriend, Caroline. They had only been seeing each other for six weeks but Dan feels bad about the break-up. Karl has since heard Caroline saying mean things about Dan, but he hasn't told Dan because he's afraid it will upset him.

    (i)   Should Karl: speak up ☐   walk away ☐   tell someone ☐?

    (ii) Explain the reason for your answer.

    _____

    _____

(d) Ciara is very fussy about everything. Her hair, clothes and accessories have to be just right. She likes pointing out how different she is to Alice, who is anything but neat and tidy. Alice doesn't want to focus on her appearance all the time. She hates when Ciara does this to her – she just wants to do normal 'friend' stuff. But she doesn't bring it up with Ciara in case she won't want to hang around with her any more.

    (i)   Should Alice: speak up ☐   walk away ☐   tell someone ☐?

    (ii) Explain the reason for your answer.

    _____

    _____

(e) Jack and Ryan walk to school together regularly. Ryan has recently told Jack that a girl in school called Nicola is having a hard time settling in. She's just moved here from another country and English is not her first language. Nicola feels unwelcome in the school and walks around on her own. Ryan wants to help her, but Jack tells him to ignore her – she's not his problem.

(i)   Should Ryan: speak up ☐   walk away ☐   tell someone ☐?

(ii) Explain the reason for your answer.

_____

_____

(f) Darina is always chatting while her friend Cynthia tends to just laugh along. Recently they have started hanging around with a group of boys and Darina keeps telling them things about Cynthia that she thinks will get a laugh. Cynthia is furious with Darina.

(i)   Should Cynthia: speak up ☐   walk away ☐   tell someone ☐?

(ii) Explain the reason for your answer.

_____

_____

The statements in the previous activity required some sort of action to be taken: to speak up, walk away or tell someone who could help. You were asked for your opinion on how to deal with such situations. If you trust your own response, then you are probably relying on the values you were taught growing up. If your decision was influenced by what you think your peer group would do, then you are passing that decision onto something that is outside of yourself. Following a peer group gives very little room for individual opinion and control. Giving in to peer pressure can really crush your independence.

NOTE
Your peers are people of your own age, e.g. your schoolmates. Peer pressure is when your peers try to influence how you act or persuade you to do something.

2. Bullying: what it is and how to cope with it

ACTIVITY

 CSPE WB1 WB2

1 What is and isn't bullying?

Read through the following statements and tick whether you think they do or do not describe bullying behaviours.

Statement	Is this a bullying incident?		Class verdict
	Yes	**No**	
(a) During maths class Clara borrowed Lisa's markers without asking because she didn't have her own with her.			
(b) Harry's basketball coach always shouts at him in front of the whole team when he misses a basket. His coach's favourite phrase is 'Stop acting the eejit, Harry!'			
(c) Jason and Paul were great friends in primary school but have drifted apart in secondary school. Paul now hangs around with a new group of boys who never speak to Jason. At break times, Paul races past Jason to get to his locker first and blocks Jason from using his locker.			
(d) Tracy often asks Kate for her phone to make calls to her other friends after school. Tracy makes arrangements to meet up with these people but never invites Kate to join in.			
(e) Karla has won lots of academic awards over the years and she always seems to know the answers to questions in every class. Recently, whenever she gives the correct answer a hissing sound can be heard from a group of students at the back of the room.			

Statement	Is this a bullying incident?		Class verdict
	Yes	No	
(f) Lorna was walking to her class when Eva walked past her in the other direction and her bag bumped off Lorna. Lorna's books fell out of her arms and onto the floor. Eva kept on walking.			
(g) Lucy passes a group of teenagers regularly on her way home. They have never spoken to her but as she passes them they all go quiet and look at her. After she passes they sometimes start laughing.			
(h) Katie loves taking photos at parties and putting them on WhatsApp and Instagram. Last week she put up a picture of Sylvia with a funny expression on her face. Now some kids are pulling that face at Sylvia and laughing; other kids are calling her a loser.			
(i) John was late getting his permission letter to his French teacher and missed the closing date for the school's French exchange trip. The teacher says he can't go now. John thinks this is unfair because a lot of his friends are going.			
(j) In geography class the teacher asked, 'Can anyone explain what hard water is?' Sophie piped up, 'Ice!' The whole class laughed but Sophie didn't understand why.			
(k) Kevin is not very good at sport – he simply has no interest in it. Because he always asks to sit out of PE lessons the other boys have started calling him girls' names. It is obvious that these names make him very upset, so the boys think this is a great source of fun.			
(l) David started in a new school after the midterm. He is from the Ivory Coast and is fluent in French but is very shy when asked to speak it in French class. Whenever he does speak French, a group of boys snigger and make fun of him. Some of the boys wait for him outside after school and push and shove him.			
(m) There is always banter and slagging going on at the lockers in the morning before assembly. This morning the banter was about Grace breaking the heel of one of her high-heel shoes when it got stuck in a drain. Her friends told everyone about it and they were all laughing. Grace was laughing too. By the end of the school day no one was really talking about it anymore.			

(a)   Compare answers with the person beside you.

(b)   Compare your answers as a class and record the verdict in the table on pages 53 and 54.

(c)   How easy or difficult did you find it to define bullying?

(d)   Was there a consensus (agreement) in your class on what is considered bullying behaviour?

_____

_____

_____

The roles of participants and bystanders in incidents of bullying

> ❝ He who passively accepts evil is as much involved in it as he who helps to perpetrate it. He who accepts evil without protesting against it is really cooperating with it. ❞
>
> *Martin Luther King, Jr*

> ❝ What if the kid you bullied at school, grew up, and turned out to be the only surgeon who could save your life? ❞
>
> *Lynette Mather, American author*

NOTE
If you witness or are experiencing bullying TELL SOMEONE you trust.

A **bystander** is someone who does not get involved when someone else needs help. Bystanders are aware of what is going on in bullying situations and in some cases become **participants**.

Participant roles

- **Assistants** who join in and assist the bully
- **Reinforcers** who do not actively attack the victim but give positive feedback to the bully, providing an audience by laughing and making other encouraging gestures
- **Outsiders** who stay away, not taking sides with anyone or being involved but allowing the bullying to continue by their 'silent approval'
- **Defenders** who show anti-bullying behaviour, comforting the victim, taking their side and trying to stop the bullying

('Bystanders and Bullying', www.anti-bullyingalliance.org.uk)

The behaviour of bystanders can be easier to change than the behaviour of bullies. A bully rarely continues to bully without his supporters and audience.

What can bystanders do?

- **Prevention:** Raise awareness of everyone's responsibility to help and support others. This promotes a culture where it is OK to ask for help.
- **Reaction:** Do something, e.g. tell a teacher.
- **Support:** Offer help to the victim and let them know you do not agree with bullying.

Remember!

The opposite of bullying is friendship.

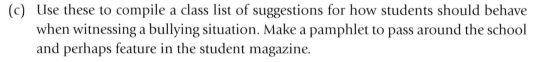
End of Module Review

(a) Divide into small groups and discuss ways in which you could change the role of bystanders when they see bullying happening.

(b) Write each group's suggestions on a piece of paper and then hang the papers on the wall.

(c) Use these to compile a class list of suggestions for how students should behave when witnessing a bullying situation. Make a pamphlet to pass around the school and perhaps feature in the student magazine.

Module 6
Relationships and Sexuality Education

This module gives you the opportunity to revise aspects of human reproduction that you may be familiar with from your Science and Home Economics classes. We will also look at the social and emotional impact of relationships.

 Digital Resources are available for this module at mentorbooks.ie/resources

We will explore:

1. From conception to birth

TRB

WB1

WB2

WB3

This section will investigate how a baby is formed. Some of the terminology (words) used may be new to you as well.

Sexual intercourse

When an adult couple are in a loving, committed relationship, they will show their love for each other in a physical way. This is known as sexual intercourse or copulation. When intercourse occurs, the male penis fills with blood and becomes erect. The erect penis is placed in the female vagina. Semen (a mixture of sperm cells and seminal fluid) is ejaculated or released into the vagina. There are about 100 million sperm in each ejaculation.

👉 **Remember!**

In *Minding Me 1: My Well-Being,* Module 6 we studied the male and female reproductive organs.

Journey of the sperm

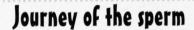

2. Fertilisation occurs in the fallopian tube if the egg meets the sperm cell

3. The fertilised egg divides and moves towards the uterus

WB3

1. An egg leaves the ovary and passes into the fallopian tube

4. The embryo becomes lodged in the prepared lining of the uterus

Sperm cells travel up from the vagina

The sperm swim up from the vagina through the cervix into the uterus and eventually up to the fallopian tubes. If there is no egg in the fallopian tube, the sperm will die within 72 hours.

Fertilisation

If there is an egg in the fallopian tube, one of the sperm cells may fuse (or join) with it. Fertilisation takes place when the nucleus of an egg fuses with the nucleus of a sperm cell to form a single cell called a **zygote**. This cell will keep multiplying and will eventually become a baby. Fertilisation takes place in the fallopian tube. Once fertilisation takes place, the woman is pregnant.

Pregnancy

Once the zygote is formed, it divides many times to become an **embryo**. The embryo takes between four and seven days to reach the uterus. The embryo then attaches itself to the lining of the uterus.

The embryo develops inside the uterus in a protective sac called the amnion. To protect the developing embryo further, this sac is filled with amniotic fluid. From week eight onwards, the embryo is called a **foetus**.

NOTE
The attachment of the embryo to the lining of the uterus is called implantation.

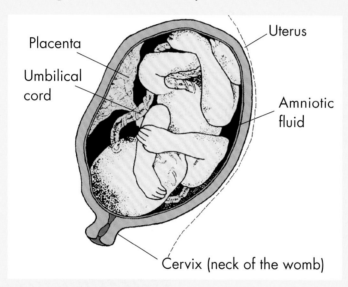

NOTE
Pregnancy is the length of time the baby spends growing and developing in the uterus (9 months, or 40 weeks).

- The embryo is connected to the placenta by means of the umbilical cord.
- The placenta is like a life-support machine for the baby and is rich in blood vessels.
- Food and oxygen pass from the mother to the baby through the placenta.
- Wastes such as carbon dioxide pass from the baby to the mother, again through the placenta.

ACTIVITY

(1) **Pregnancy**

(a) Can you think of substances other than food or oxygen that may pass from mother to foetus?

_____

(b) The mother's blood and the baby's blood never mix. Why do you think this is?

_____

Development of a baby in pregnancy

WB3

Week	Stage of development
Week 1	Fertilisation and implantation of embryo occur.
Week 2	Placenta, eyes and limbs of embryo begin to form.
Week 8	All organs are formed. Embryo is called a foetus.
Week 14	Sex of foetus can be determined.
Week 16–18	Mother can feel movements of foetus.
Week 28	Baby turns upside down so that the head is near the cervix.
Week 38	Baby is fully developed and ready to be born.

NOTE
Watch Alexander
Tsiaras's TED Talk
'Conception to Birth –
visualized'
(www.ted.com).

Birth

- The birth of the baby begins when the muscles of the uterus begin to contract. This is known as labour.
- The woman's waters break. This means the amniotic sac bursts to release the amniotic fluid through the vagina.
- The contractions continue to widen the cervix to ten centimetres.
- Eventually the baby is pushed head first through the cervix and the vagina. The umbilical cord is clamped and cut.
- The baby then breathes, using its lungs for the first time.
- Some babies are delivered by a caesarean section (C-section), which is a surgical incision in the mother's abdomen and uterus. This method of delivery can be planned or used to assist in situations where the baby cannot be delivered through the birth canal.

On a ruler, measure 10 centimetres. This is the size to which the cervix must widen to allow a baby to push through into the vagina.

2. Recognising and expressing feelings and emotions

Emotions control your thinking, behaviour and actions. Positive emotions release hormones from the brain to make a person feel good. Negative emotions, if not recognised and dealt with, can be carried around in the body as stress. People who ignore, dismiss or repress their emotions may end up suffering a physical illness.

TRB

WB1

ACTIVITY

a b c
d e f
g h

1 Good and bad days

A good day

Imagine a day starting off at a normal pace. You arrive on time to school and receive greetings from your friends as you go from lesson to lesson. Then you get a test back from your Maths teacher, who is clearly impressed

with your progress. The positive emotions you experience are contentment and feeling valued.

A bad day

Now imagine a day starting off at a frantic pace. You rush to school while eating a slice of toast, then trip over your laces, get butter on your trousers and all your classmates laugh at you. You

push your way to your locker for class materials after each class, to the annoyance of fellow students. Then you get a test back from your Maths teacher, who is clearly unimpressed with your lack of progress.

(a) What emotions would you experience on the bad day?

_____

_____

(b) Do you think it is important to talk about those emotions? Why/why not?

_____

_____

(c) What do you think is the moral of these two stories?

_____

_____

> ‘ When you reach for the stars, you are reaching for the farthest thing out there. When you reach deep into yourself, it is the same thing, but in the opposite direction. If you reach in both directions, you will have spanned the universe. ’
>
> Vera Nazarian, The Perpetual Calendar of Inspiration

Recognising how you are feeling at a given time is the first step to accepting how it is affecting you. Labelling the feeling is very useful, e.g. 'I am feeling resentful' or 'I am feeling frightened'. You can then choose how you wish to express that feeling. Your feelings are your inner voice telling you how you are experiencing a situation.

Your inner voice can also be the warning signal that you may be in a dangerous situation – this can lead to the 'fight or flight' reaction. Your body builds up adrenalin to stay and fight or to run away from whatever danger lies in wait. While nowadays we don't need to defend ourselves from hungry animals who see us as prey, we still face challenges to our personal safety. Images we see on social media and characters we watch in shows or films can make us feel under pressure to look and behave in the same way. We feel peer pressure to do things that we don't really want to do, and we fear that we will be mocked if we look or behave differently.

Romantic relationships

There are many misconceptions about how people should behave in romantic relationships and this can confuse young people's understanding of a healthy and realistic relationship. Soap operas and romantic movies do not illustrate a healthy expression of love – they need drama, betrayal and mistrust to keep the viewers watching. But healthy and happy relationships are not constantly packed with drama and betrayal.

2 **Is this what it really feels like to fall in love?**

(a) Read the following statements about falling in love and tick whether you agree, disagree or are unsure about the statements.

Statement	Agree	Disagree	Unsure
(i) Love is blind.			
(ii) Love starts off being difficult.			
(iii) Love is something that one person must fight for and never give up on.			
(iv) Love allows for both people to change and grow.			
(v) Love always means living happily ever after.			
(vi) Love is knowing who the right person is for you as soon as you meet.			
(vii) Love is making promises to each other that you both must keep.			
(viii) Love means respecting that you might have different interests.			

(b) What do you think love is?

_____

_____

3 **Emotional readiness**

With your partner, discuss the following questions.

(a) What does it mean to be emotionally ready for a romantic relationship?

(b) Do you think you will recognise when you're emotionally ready for a romantic relationship?

(c) What emotions will be challenged in a romantic relationship?

Spending time with people who you like and who like you in return as well as spending time doing activities that you enjoy will help you to stay true to who you are. In your life, try to demonstrate the values and characteristics that you would expect from close friends. Work on your goals and ambitions, be open to involving people along the way but remember to stay true to yourself.

3. Peer pressure and other influences

Our peers are a huge part of our lives and we all like to feel that we are part of a group. But sometimes we may feel pressured by that group into doing something we don't want to do. So how can we hold on to our individuality and resist peer pressure?

1 **The influence of peer pressure**

Discuss the following statements with your partner.

(a) Peer pressure can be positive as well as negative.

(b) Peer pressure can influence us in a number of ways.

Paired ACTIVITY

(2) **What can you do about peer pressure?**

With your partner, imagine you were advising a younger brother or sister about how to resist giving in to peer pressure from a group of friends in school who don't seem to care about his/her well-being.

(a) What strategies would you recommend?

(b) What pressures do you think should be reported and how would you recommend getting help?

(c) What advice would you give about the value of keeping your individuality?

Sexting

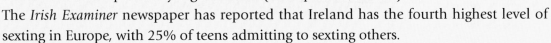

TRB

What is it? 'Sexting' is a term used to describe the sharing of sexually explicit images or videos to another person by digital media (smartphones, tablets).

The *Irish Examiner* newspaper has reported that Ireland has the fourth highest level of sexting in Europe, with 25% of teens admitting to sexting others.

Group ACTIVITY

(3) **Class discussion**

Why do you think people send or want to receive sexts?

Amanda Todd's story

WB1 **WB2**

Fifteen-year-old Amanda Todd took her own life at her home in British Columbia, Canada, in October 2012. The start of her emotional breakdown was a topless photo that was taken of her without her knowledge. She agreed to 'flash' the guy she was 'chatting' to online but she didn't know he was taking a picture of her. Before she took her own life she posted a video on YouTube of herself holding up flashcards that described her experience of being blackmailed to expose her breasts via webcam and the consequences afterwards of being bullied and assaulted. Amanda didn't tell anyone this was happening to her at the time. Her mother, Carol Todd, now dedicates her time to raising awareness about the issues that affected Amanda. She believes in telling young people about what can happen online. She stresses the point that we all make mistakes – it is a normal part of growing up – so it is okay to ask for help and talk to a trusted adult.

For more information about Amanda's story visit amandatoddlegacy.org

ACTIVITY

4 **What do you think?**

(a) Reflect on Amanda's story and write your thoughts below.

_____

_____

(b) How did Amanda's story make you feel?

_____

_____

(c) Why do you think Amanda exposed her breasts to someone on the computer?

_____

_____

(d) Amanda didn't know the pictures were being taken so she wasn't deliberately sexting. Do you think it matters to the person in the picture if they are deliberately sexting or the sexts happen accidentally?

_____

_____

(e) What do you think prevented her from getting help when the situation got out of control?

_____

_____

(f) How would you have helped her if you were Amanda's friend?

_____

_____

5 **Using your phone?**

(a) How often do you send texts or pictures via your phone?

_____

_____

(b) Have you ever sent a photo of a person without their permission? Do you think this is okay?

_____

_____

(c) Have you ever received a text or image that upset you? If yes, what did you do?

_____

_____

(d) Have you ever received a text or image that was of a sexual nature? If yes, what did you do?

_____

_____

WB2

Group ACTIVITY

6 **Saying no to sexts**

In groups, come up with three ways to turn down a request for a sext. Two examples are given to start you off.

(a)

I can't send you nude photos, but I'll forward this request to my dad and you can ask him.

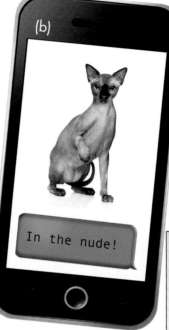

(b)

In the nude!

NOTE
Check out an app called Send This Instead, launched by the Ontario Provincial Police Child Sexual Exploitation Unit to help teens cope with the pressure of being asked to send a sext.

'I'd rather be called a prude than for my granny to receive a sext of me in the nude!'

✂ **Remember!**

Ask yourself, 'Do I really need to send a naked picture of myself in the first place?'

Helpful websites:
www.thinkuknow.co.uk
www.b4udecide.ie
www.SpunOut.ie

What can you do if you regret sending a sext?

1. Don't panic. Talk to a trusted adult or friend and ask for their help. There are a lot of places you can go to for help, support and advice from trained professionals in school, your community or the websites listed on this page.

2. If you are on good terms with the person you sent the sext to, ask them to delete it as soon as you can. The quicker you do something the less chance of further distress.

3. Contact the service provider directly. Most social media sites have ways of blocking users from contacting you and departments where you can report abuse on the site.

4. If you receive someone else's embarrassing picture, do not forward it or share it with anyone else: 'Delete and don't repeat'. Put yourself in that person's shoes and imagine how they are feeling. Let a trusted adult know about the situation and remember there are legal consequences of having such images on your device. Sending or receiving a sexually suggestive text or image, especially if a person is under 17 years of age (even if it is you sending or receiving the image), is considered 'child exploitation material' and can result in criminal charges.

5. Although there is no guarantee that the images will be deleted on the Internet, or that future employees or boyfriends or girlfriends won't find out about your pictures, you can still exercise some control by deciding to be honest and upfront with people you meet in the future. Remember the words of Amanda Todd's mother: 'Making mistakes is normal and part of growing up'. It will be the things you have done since then that will show that there is so much more to you.

4. Making responsible decisions

WB1

WB2

WB4

From learning about peer pressure, we can see how each person has a responsibility to form their own attitudes, beliefs and values about relationships and how to function in them. The attitudes and beliefs that a person develops can be based on those they have received from parents, mentors or their religious faith.

Paired
ACTIVITY

WB1

WB4

1 **Types of relationships**

Examine the pictures above and discuss your interpretation with your partner, using the following questions:

(a) What do you think the word relationship means?

_____

_____

(b) Discuss the many different kinds of relationships people share.

_____

_____

2. Important features of a relationship

(a) In pairs, brainstorm the features or values that contribute to establishing a healthy relationship, e.g. respect, understanding.

(b) As a class, agree on nine values and list them on the board.

(c) In smaller groups decide the order in which the nine values should be placed in one large diamond, where the most important feature of a relationship is at the top, the two second most important on the next row down and so on until the least important feature appears on the bottom.

(d) When your group's diamond nine is complete, copy it into the diagram below.

Aware

WB1

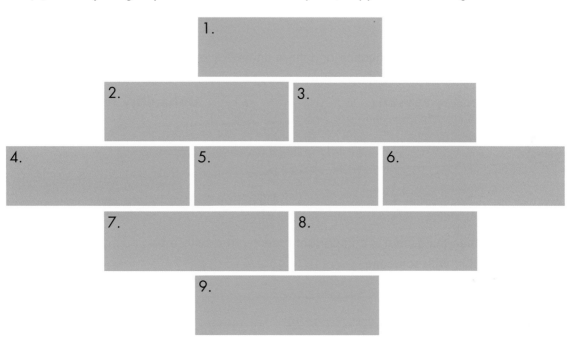

(e) Discuss the following.

   (i) How easy or difficult was it to decide on values with one other person?

   (ii) As a group, how did you decide on the nine values to list?

   (iii) When it came to doing the diamond nine, what guided your discussion and decisions about how you would rank the nine values you had chosen?

   (iv) Were there differences among those in the group? Why/why not?

Everyone has different values that guide their attitudes and behaviour in relationships. It is important to be aware of our values when we are making decisions in relationships and to respect other people's values, which may be different from our own, particularly in our personal relationships. When we make a decision that is in line with our own personal values, it is more likely that it will be a healthy one for us.

(Adapted from *Relationships and Sexuality Education: Resource Materials for Teachers*, b4udecide.ie)

5. Health and personal safety

TRB

1 Brainstorm

(a) Why do you think people have sex?

(i) _____

(ii) _____

(iii) _____

(iv) _____

(b) Can you identify three healthy and three unhealthy reasons to have sex?

Healthy reasons	Unhealthy reasons
(i)	(i)
(ii)	(ii)
(iii)	(iii)

(c) Name three things that are important to remember before beginning a sexual relationship with someone.

(i) _____

(ii) _____

(iii) _____

2 Class discussion

Although the human body is ready to create a baby in the teenage years, are teenagers emotionally ready to have a baby? What do you think?

It is up to you to decide when you feel ready to start having sex, but you should not let anyone pressure you into having a sexual relationship.

Remember!

If you are under the age of 17, anyone having sex with you is breaking the law. If you are 17 or over, then you are breaking the law if you have sex with someone under the age of 17 – even if the sex is consenual. Even though the legal age of consent in Ireland is 17, this does not mean that you are ready to have sex at age 17 – *you* decide when you feel ready.

CSPE

Safety

The risks young people take in certain relationships can impact on them for the rest of their lives. Sexual intercourse at a young age can lead to unplanned pregnancies and sexually transmitted infections (STIs), e.g. HIV/AIDS.

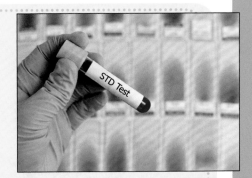

TRB

WB3

STI facts
• STIs can be passed from one person to the next through sexual contact including sexual intercourse.
• According to the HSE's Health Prevention Surveillance Centre, there are 7.5 diagnoses of HIV per 100,000 population in Ireland each year.
• Abstinence from close/intimate sexual contact is the only way to give yourself 100% protection against unplanned pregnancy and STIs. Most unplanned pregnancies result from unprotected sex or not using contraception properly.
• Condoms, when used correctly, offer protection against most STIs. No other method of contraception provides protection against STIs.
• STIs are caused by bacteria and viruses which can be found in blood, semen and bodily fluids.
• Some STIs can lead to infertility and certain cancers.
• Alcohol or illicit drugs are often involved when people catch an STI – they lower inhibitions and cloud the ability to judge safe sexual activity from irresponsible sex.
• During 2013, a total of 12,753 cases of sexually transmitted infections (STIs) were reported in Ireland.

End of Module Review

Fill in the blanks.

1. Fertilisation of the egg with sperm in the female body occurs in the f_____ tube.

2. When the nucleus of an egg fuses with the nucleus of the sperm cell it forms a single cell called a z_____.

3. Food and oxygen pass from the mother to the baby through the p_____

4. The age of consent for sexual activity in Ireland is _____ years of age.

5. The letters STI stand for S_____T_____I_____

Module 7
Emotional Health

This module will explore what a realistic, positive body image is and how self-confidence and body image can support each other.

 Digital Resources are available for this module at mentorbooks.ie/resources

We will explore:

1. Self-confidence

1 **Remember**

In Module 2 we looked at self-confidence. List three things you remember about self-confidence.

(a) _____

(b) _____

(c) _____

Other people's comments and behaviour can influence the way we feel about ourselves. These comments can be called **external affirmations** – i.e. they come from outside, from other people. Depending on whether the external affirmation is positive or negative, our feelings about ourselves, our abilities and our appearance can be good or bad. These feelings are channelled into positive or negative emotions, e.g. pride or irritation.

2 **External affirmations**

(a) In the table below, tick one negative and one positive personal comment.

	Positive	Negative
(i) That is a very good idea.		
(ii) Well, you were never good at maths, were you?		
(iii) Your brother would never have done that!		
(iv) You seem to have grasped that idea well.		
(v) Do not make a show of yourself by asking stupid questions.		
(vi) Typical girl.		
(vii) You stupid boy!		

(b) Describe how one of the positive comments would make you feel.

You feel like you can do it

(c) Describe the effect that one of the negative comments could have on an individual's self-confidence.

You feel like you can't do it and so you give up

WB1

High and low self-confidence

- Self-confidence is a positive and personal sense of your capabilities.
- Having **high** self-confidence means that you have a positive opinion of yourself and that you feel good about your personality and your physical self.
- Having **low** self-confidence means that you have a negative opinion of yourself and that you may feel little self-worth. You may even have negative feelings about your physical self.

Aware

3 ## High or low?

Rate each item listed in the table below from 1 to 6, with 1 being the lowest and 6 being the highest, as to whether you feel you have high self-confidence or low self-confidence in it. Answer as honestly as possible.

⇐ **Low self-confidence**   **High self-confidence** ⇒

		1	2	3	4	5	6
A	My intelligence						
B	My opinions and beliefs						
C	My self-worth						
D	My abilities						
E	My communication skills						
F	My body language						
G	My social skills						
H	My ambition						
I	My place in the world						
J	My physical appearance						

It would be most unusual if you scored highly in all areas; nobody is perfect. However, look at the areas where you did score highly – is there a pattern?

If you scored highly with the more personal values (numbers A–D), then you possess inner confidence. A high score in the more social values (numbers E, G and I) means you possess outer confidence. It might be a good idea to think of a slogan or mantra that will boost your confidence in areas where you scored low for self-confidence or to practise skills in this area, starting with something small. For example, to improve social skills you could try talking to a group of people you don't know well.

A balance of personal and social values will certainly build your self-esteem and help you to take on the challenges of life.

ACTIVITY

4 **Looking at the positives (in you)**

Fill in the blank spaces below:

(a) Name

_____

(b) Three best personal qualities (e.g. good listener, loyal)

(i) _____

(ii) _____

(iii) _____

(c) Three of your talents (e.g. dancing, fixing things etc.)

(i) _____

(ii) _____

(iii) _____

(d) Three of your best physical features (e.g. height, teeth, dimples etc.)

(i) _____

(ii) _____

(iii) _____

(e) Three of your successes so far (e.g. ignoring a bully, learning a very difficult poem, competitions etc.)

(i) _____

(ii) _____

(iii) _____

(f) Three examples of your ability to rise to a challenge (e.g. joining your school's debating team, taking part in a charity run etc.)

(i) _____

(ii) _____

(iii) _____

(g) Your future ambitions

(i) _____

(ii) _____

(iii) _____

Keep this page safe – you don't need to share it with anyone. Remember to look at it when you need to reassure yourself that you are a great person.

2. Body image

WB1

TRB

The term body image is used to describe the way we see our own body. We recognise this image of ourselves from a very young age. Young children look in the mirror and love to see themselves. However, as children grow into pre-teens and teenagers, their image of themselves can often become distorted or less positive than before.

ACTIVITY

1 **Influences**

Can you name three things that might influence a pre-teen or teenager to change the way they see themselves or their body image?

(a) _____

(b) _____

(c) _____

Our body image and our self-worth can often be interlinked and can change throughout our lives. If a person receives positive or negative feedback about their appearance this can influence the way they feel about themselves.

WB2

2 **Case study**

Jane is 14 and was really excited about going to summer camp with her friends for the first time. She had recently lost three stone in weight and was feeling really positive about herself – she loved the new Jane. On the first night of the camp a boy from another school made a reference to Jane's size and said that she should eat more and exercise less. Jane felt really upset and didn't want to join in the activities over the next few days. Instead she spent her time alone. Jane's friends didn't know what had happened to the new Jane …

(a) Why is Jane feeling the way she is?

_____

_____

(b) What can Jane's friends do?

_____

_____

(c) What advice would you give Jane?

_____

_____

_____

3 **The media**

(a) As a class, use magazines and newspapers to create two collages to display in your classroom on the following topics:
(i) Images of women in the media.
(ii) Images of men in the media.

(b) While working on each collage, find words to describe how each gender is depicted in the media today. Attach these words to each collage.

(c) What stereotypical male and female imagery have come to your attention?

	Male	Female
Face		
Body		
Mood/emotion		
Environment/scene		

Positive body image

It is important to know that people can dislike parts of their body, e.g. nose, feet etc., but still have an overall positive body image. A positive or negative body image is linked to the way a person behaves or acts.

Negative body image becomes a problem when:
- The way you look influences your social situations, your work and your relationships.
- You believe you can only feel confident or be happy by changing the way you look.
- You believe that the way you look is preventing you from taking part in certain activities.
- You are always worrying about your appearance.
- You repeatedly check your appearance in a full-length mirror.
- You consistently use very heavy make-up even when playing sport.
- You refuse to leave the house without product in your hair.
- You won't go out without make-up on.

Teenagers with a **healthy body image**:
- Recognise that bodies come in all shapes and sizes.
- Can name the good things about their own body.
- Are comfortable with their own bodies.
- Know there's no such thing as the perfect body.

4 **This is me**

Make a collage using selected pictures, words, drawings and other things you like that, when put together, say 'This is me'.

- Focus on the qualities you possess.
- Include the events or achievements of which you are most proud.
- Attach pictures of activities, hobbies and dressing styles that you like.

Paired ACTIVITY

5 **Influences on body image**

Our body image and how we see ourselves can be influenced by the following:

Family   **Friends**   **Society**   **Media**

With your partner, discuss one way in which each group of people can influence your body image from an early age.

❝I am the only me I've got and I am unique. There are two major parts of me. There is the inside me and the outside me. ❞

'Everybody is somebody', The Body Image Project Tool Kit

ACTIVITY

6 **Body expression**

Do you agree or disagree with the following statements. Explain the reason for your answer.

Statement	Agree/Disagree	Why?
(a) The clothes we wear can affect how we feel about ourselves.		
(b) How we feel can influence the clothes we decide to wear.		
(c) How other people react to what we wear can influence how we feel.		

7 **What I wear and why**

(a) Pick the five pieces of clothing which you wear the most often. Describe how these make you feel and why.

	Clothing	Feeling	Why?
(i)			
(ii)			
(iii)			
(iv)			
(v)			

(b) What would cause you to stop wearing them?

_____

_____

_____

_____

We are all unique

WB4

All of us are unique in our own way. There are things that we love about ourselves and things we might like to change. It's important to remember that we have no control over many things, and we have to learn to accept them in ourselves and in other people. Some things we can change with a bit of effort and some things will change over time, as we live our lives and gain experience.

8 **Differences**

Think about the differences between people. In the bubbles below, write a difference that we can't change, a difference we can change with effort and a difference that can change with time.

Can't change

height

Can change with effort

increase fitness

Can change with time

presence/absence of wisdom teeth

9 **Advertising and body image**

(a) Does the ad below include people of different sizes?

_____

(b) Do you think most people who use this product regularly look like the models?

_____

(c) Do you think the people in this ad are happy?

_____

BEST BURGER – THE BEST PART OF THE DAY!

WB2

10 Discussion points

(a) In small groups, discuss the following statements to explore how different people feel about what a positive body image is.

   (i) Name a fad diet (i.e. promises quick weight loss through unhealthy and unbalanced diet).

   (ii) Who is your role model and why?

   (iii) Identify a way your family affects your body image.

   (iv) Who can make us feel good about our body image?

   (v) What makes a healthy body?

   (vi) Can healthy bodies come in all shapes and sizes?

   (vii) Do body ideals change over time?

   (viii) Do you think most real people look like fashion models?

   (ix) Name one thing about your body that you feel good about.

   (x) Who can make us feel bad about our bodies?

(b) Following the discussion, each group should pick one statement and make a two-minute presentation about it to the class.

End of Module Review

(a) Thinking back on what was explored in this module, fill in the table below.

What did you learn about body image?	What did you learn about self-confidence?

(b) A personal goal to work on over the next month would be:

_____

_____

_____

Module 8
Influences and decisions

You learned a number of key skills in *Minding Me 1: My Well-Being* and the earlier modules in this book, including organisational skills (Module 2) and communication skills (Module 3). In this module, we will continue to build your life skills.

 Digital Resources are available for this module at mentorbooks.ie/resources

We will explore:

1. Positive and negative influences

Just as young people have role models who will influence their behaviour in positive ways, young people can also have role models who might have a negative influence on them. This negative influence can result in a young person experimenting with drink or drugs, cheating or avoiding exams and assignments in school or engaging in bullying behaviour. Often young people may find themselves in situations with friends where peer pressure is encouraging this negative behaviour. Having **one good adult** to talk to can help a young person to avoid or move on from such situations.

One good adult

We know that the presence of one good adult in a young person's life has a positive influence on their mental health. Be it a parent, teacher, sports coach or school bus driver, all adults have a role in supporting the young people around them.

NOTE
Watch Danny Nee's short film *One Good Adult* on YouTube. It features young people speaking about what their one good adults have meant to them.

1 **My one good adult**
Who is your one good adult? Why do you find it so easy to speak to them? Why do you listen to their opinion?

Name: _____

Why he/she is my one good adult:

(a) _____

_____

(b) _____

_____

(c) _____

_____

(d) _____

_____

(e) _____

_____

Maintaining your well-being

❝Never get tired of doing little things for others; sometimes those little things occupy the biggest part of our hearts❞

www.enlightening quotes.com

Below is a list of five things you can do every day to help maintain your well-being throughout your life.

Maintain relationships: Relationships take time to build so allow yourself the time every day to connect with your family, friends, neighbours etc.

Set goals: This is really for your motivation and sense of achievement throughout your life. This could be about studying for your exams or assessments, but you might also want to learn to dance or play a musical instrument or play a new sport. Set that goal and join the class.

Keep active: Activity is a vital part of our overall well-being. It doesn't have to be about going to the gym – it could be playing a sport, going for a walk each day or learning yoga. Make this activity part of your life and ensure it is something you enjoy doing.

Be grateful: Even if everything isn't as you might like it to be, be thankful for what you have. Give back to those around you and people you meet: say hello, smile, give a kind word or do something nice, e.g. hold the door open for someone. Engage in larger acts of giving by volunteering in your community, e.g. visiting elderly patients in your local hospital, joining your local Tidy Towns organisation etc. All of this will help your well-being, as it is often through giving to others that we start to feel better about ourselves.

Practise mindfulness: Be aware of the present moment and what you are doing, what is around you. Doing this every day – either in the morning or before you go to sleep – allows you the time to be aware of your thoughts and feelings from the day or about the day ahead. But remember it does take practice: start with four to five minutes and build from there.

❝Be thankful for what you have; you'll end up having more. If you concentrate on what you don't have, you will never, ever have enough.❞

Oprah Winfrey

2 **Maintaining my well-being**

Write down what you will do each day to maintain your well-being in the areas listed in the table below.

Maintain relationships	
Set goals	
Keep active	
Be grateful	
Practise mindfulness	

TRB

By keeping your mind healthy and well and by linking with people who can positively influence your life, you will be happier and more content.

 Remember!

Maintaining your well-being is something you will learn – it does not happen without hard work and effort.

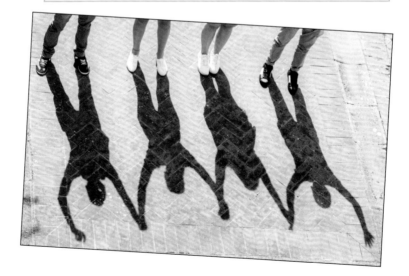

2. Making decisions

TRB

1 Big decisions/small decisions

> Should I take a cigarette the next time Tommy offers me one?

> How can I avoid meeting up with Mary?

> What will I have for dinner?

> I am worried my mum and dad will break up.

> I haven't studied for my exam.

> Teresa was looking at me today and whispering. I am worried she is saying mean things about me.

> I stole money from my granny's purse. Why did I do that?

All of these thoughts are important to the person thinking them.

(a) Can you circle the thoughts that might require you to confide in your one good adult?

(b) Are there any that you might be able to make a decision on by yourself?

Just how do we make decisions?

We usually weigh up a decision by looking at the pros and cons (**pro** means 'for' and **con** means 'against' in Latin). It is actually quite a complex process which requires us to reflect before, during and after the decision.

There are many ways of coming to a decision. On the next page we will look at the Plus Minus Implications (PMI) model, developed by psychologist Edward de Bono. Place a tick beside any thoughts you think you could tackle alone.

Using PMI

(a) A three-column table is used with the headings 'plus', 'minus' and 'implications'.

Plus	Minus	Implications

(b) All the positives linked to making the decision will be listed in the 'plus' column. They can be scored from +1 to +5.

+1	+2	+3	+4	+5
Least positive				Most positive

(c) All the negatives linked to making the decision will be listed in the 'minus' column. They can be scored from -1 to -5.

-1	-2	-3	-4	-5
Least negative				Most negative

(d) All the consequences linked to making the decision will be listed in the 'implications' column. Positive consequences can be scored from +1 to +5.

+1	+2	+3	+4	+5
Least positive				Most positive

Negative consequences can be scored from -1 to -5.

-1	-2	-3	-4	-5
Least negative				Most negative

(e) Once you have written down the pluses, minuses and implications of your possible decision and scored them, add up the score. A strongly positive score suggests the action should be taken, whereas a strongly negative score suggests that it might be better to avoid it.

A sample PMI approach

Read Denis's letter to his one good adult and look at the PMI table Denis used to help him make his decision.

Dear Uncle Kevin,
My best friend has started smoking. She really wants me to try it too. I don't know what to do. I really hate smoking and it will probably affect my basketball, but I am afraid I will lose my friend if I don't try it.
Denis, 14

Decision:

If Denis chooses to smoke …

Plus	Minus	Implications
Best friend will think he is cool (+1)	He may feel sick when he breathes in smoke fumes (−5)	He may feel sick and will not be able to run as fast in basketball (−5)
He will still have his best friend (+5)	Breath smells, clothes smell (−5)	Get into trouble at home (−5)
	Costs a lot (−5)	
Total: +6	Total: −15	Total: −10

The table is scored:

+6 (plus) −15 (minus) −10 (implications) = −19

Result:

−19 is a negative answer. It is clear from this result that Denis should not smoke.

2 **Stephanie's decision**

Now, with your partner, try the PMI process with Stephanie's problem below.

Dear _____ (your one good adult),
I really love sport and play camogie and Gaelic football.
I train every evening after school and have matches
throughout the week. I know that I can't keep this up as I'm
not getting to see my friends and I am getting into trouble
in school over my homework. I need to figure out what
needs to go. Can you help?
Stephanie, 14

Plus	Minus	Implications
Total:	Total:	Total:

Result:

_____

The next time you have to make a decision, do this exercise and imagine what your one good adult might say. Even if you cannot talk to them at that particular moment, keep thinking about what their advice might be. This should help to keep you focused and safe from making risky and sometimes life-changing choices.

End of Module Review

My gratitude journal

On the page below, write at least five things you are grateful for today – small or big (e.g. 'I had a nice walk to school' or 'My granny is getting out of hospital').

My journal

_____

1. _____

_____

2. _____

_____

3. _____

_____

4. _____

_____

5. _____

_____

_____

Module 9
Substance Use

In this module we will look at the physical and psychological effects of legal and illegal drugs.

 Digital Resources are available for this module at mentorbooks.ie/resources

We will explore:

1. The effects of drugs

WB3

A person can become physically and psychologically dependent on any form of drug, both legal *and* illegal.

This physical and psychological dependence or addiction creates problems for people in society.

ACTIVITY

1 Definitions

(a) Physically dependent means

_____

(b) Psychologically dependent means

_____

Addiction

A person's risk of becoming addicted to a substance increases during times of change. Adolescence is a time of changing from being a child to becoming an adult. In secondary school, teenagers become aware of drugs and drugs may also be more accessible than in primary school. This is why it is important that you understand the effects on your well-being of taking drugs and know how to say no.

WB1

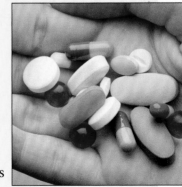

During adolescence, decision-making and judgement skills are still developing. This can result in young people deciding to experiment with drugs. However this can often lead to addiction. Sometimes young people think if a drug is legal then it must be safe, but this is not always the case. For example, alcohol and cigarettes are legal drugs that can have dangerous long-term effects on health.

ACTIVITY

2 Legal drugs

Can you name two legal drugs available for sale in Ireland which can be harmful to the body in different ways?

(a) _____

_____

(b) _____

_____

2. Legal highs — head shops

Head shops sell products advertised as 'natural' alternatives to illegal drugs. But, in reality, they are untested for human safety and can be just as dangerous as illegal drugs.

Many head-shop products were banned from sale in Ireland in 2010, which resulted in the closure of the majority of head shops in the country. However, these products are still widely available online. The psychoactive substances (which can alter the way you feel, think and behave) offered online are sold as alternatives to other illegal drugs.

NOTE
Being 'natural' doesn't make a product safe.

Side effects of head-shop products

- Confusion
- Increased risk taking
- Anxiety
- Panic attacks/paranoia
- Disturbed sleep/insomnia, resulting in exhaustion and depression
- Negative impact on mental health
- Toxic, resulting in possible damage to kidneys, coma, death

Despite the closure of many head shops in Ireland, we still have one of the highest rates of legal-high usage in Europe. When a drug is banned, manufacturers replace it quickly with another that has similar effects but is made from different chemicals. This means it's technically legal, and these new drugs are being created and sold faster than the authorities can ban them. People using these drugs often have no idea what chemicals they are taking or in what quantity. Already several deaths in Ireland have been linked to the drug 25I-NBOMe, known as N-Bomb.

 Remember!

Just because something is not technically illegal, that doesn't mean it's safe. Using these substances can have fatal consequences.

 **ACTIVITY**

 1 **KWL**
KWL stands for **Know**, **Want to know** and **Learned**. In the table below, list two things you know about the impact head-shop products could have on your health. In the second column, list two other possible impacts you'd like to learn more about. Research these and record your findings in the third column.

K	W	L

3. Anabolic steroids

WB1

There are two types of steroids:

- corticosteroids
- anabolic steroids

Corticosteroids are similar to the hormone adrenaline. They help you fight stress when you are sick or injured by reducing inflammation. Doctors can prescribe corticosteroids to treat arthritis, asthma, autoimmune diseases, skin conditions and some cancers.

Anabolic steroids are chemicals that produce similar effects to the male sex hormone testosterone. Some teenagers take steroids to alter their appearance or improve their athletic performance. Steroids can be used to increase muscle size.

 WB3

Physical effects of anabolic steroids on the body

- Steroids can cause kidney, liver and heart damage, mood swings and dependency.
- Due to the amount of testosterone-like chemicals involved, they can have a profound effect on male and female reproductive organs, which can impact on fertility later in life.
- Steroids can impair learning and memory. They can also have a strong influence on the person's mood.
- Males may develop breasts and notice testicle shrinkage. Females may develop deeper voices and see increased facial-hair growth.
- Steroid use can also lead to stunted growth, severe acne and aggressive behaviour.

ACTIVITY

1 **Case study**

Joe has returned from spending two weeks with his cousin. He can't wait to show his friends Carmel and Jim what his cousin gave him to help him get picked for the school rugby team. Joe shows the tablets to Carmel and Jim and tells them what effect the tablets will have. He tells them his cousin, who is 15 too, now looks so much bigger and is on his school team. Jim recognises these as steroids and knows the damage they can do, as he has read about it on a sports website. Carmel wants to use them so she might get picked for her team. Jim tells Joe and Carmel how dangerous steroids can be, but they tell him they are legal so it must be fine. It's not like they are drugs or anything …

Write two different endings to the above story – one where Joe and Carmel listen to Jim and one where they don't.

(a) **Friends listen:**

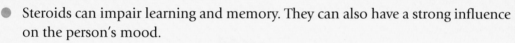

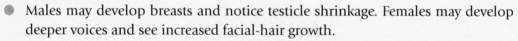

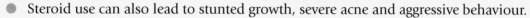

_____

(b) **Friends don't listen:**

_____

_____

_____

_____

Steroids in sport

All athletes alter their bodies in some way to improve their performance. They exercise and diet; they undergo medical treatment after injury to help them get back to competing quickly; they often remove body hair to avoid wind resistance. These behaviours are considered acceptable within the sporting world. Some athletes undergo performance-enhancing surgeries – this is a grey area and its acceptability is often debated. And some use drugs to increase muscle or allow them to train longer – this is considered cheating.

ACTIVITY

2 **Acceptable or cheating?**

Consider the examples below. Do you think these behaviours are acceptable?

Explain why/why not.

(a) A Gaelic footballer who uses an inhaler to help her compete.

_____

_____

(b) A sprinter who takes anabolic steroids.

_____

_____

4. Cannabis and its effects

What is cannabis?

- It is an illegal drug made from the _Cannabis sativa_ plant that contains 400 different chemicals.
- THC (tetrahydrocannabinol) is the chemical that causes the main effects of cannabis.
- Cannabis usually comes as dried resin (hash) or dried leaves (grass/weed).

1. **Why do people use cannabis?**

Give three reasons why you think people use cannabis.

(a)_____

(b)_____

(c)_____

Legal view

● Cannabis is illegal in Ireland, but some other countries have legalised it for medical use (e.g. Canada). In some other countries (e.g. Holland) it is legal to carry a small amount for personal use.

● It is illegal to grow, produce, supply and possess cannabis in Ireland.

● All cannabis products are controlled by the Misuse of Drugs Act. A person can be fined or receive a prison sentence depending on the quantity of cannabis in their possession or the number of times they have been convicted.

● The ban on cannabis in Ireland covers both medical and non-medical use of the drug.

2. **Why is it illegal?**

Give two reasons why you think cannabis is illegal in Ireland.

(a)_____

(b)_____

Group ACTIVITY

3. **Debate**

As a class debate the following motion:

Cannabis should never be legalised in Ireland.

After the debate, vote as a class group to uphold (i.e. agree with) the motion or oppose (i.e. disagree with) the motion.

WB3

Physical effects of cannabis use

- People may feel relaxed and uninhibited, become talkative and giddy.
- They may see colours more vibrantly and hear sounds more intensely.
- They can suffer hallucinations and poor judgement.
- Their speech may become slurred and they could suffer short-term memory loss.
- They are often incapable of driving a car or operating machinery.
- Cannabis causes lung cancer: it contains three times more carcinogenic (i.e. cancer-causing) tars than tobacco and five times more poisonous carbon monoxide.
- It causes decreased sperm count and decreased motility of sperm in males.
- It interferes with female ovulation.

Psychological effects

- People can become psychologically dependent on cannabis.
- It can kill brain cells.
- Cannabis is thought to contribute to schizophrenia and other psychological disorders.
- It can cause amotivational syndrome – this is when a person suffers from apathy (lack of interest) and lack of ambition.

Social effects

- Absenteeism from work or school
- Apathy towards schoolwork
- Poor academic performance
- Disruption of family life
- Inability to play sport well

Paired ACTIVITY

4 **'Facts about Drugs'**
With your partner, design a leaflet for young people called 'Facts about Drugs'. Present the information in a way that you think would encourage teenagers to read about the effects of drugs on the body and in society.

Helpful websites:
www.spunout.ie
www.talktofrank.com
www.drugs.ie
www.alcoholireland.ie

End of Module
Review

Design a poster based on the impact drug taking can have on a person's mental well-being.

Module 10
Personal Safety

As we grow older the level of responsibility we have for our own personal safety increases. In other words, as we grow older, we can't expect other people to look after us as much as when we were young children. It is important for everyone to be conscious of their own safety and how to protect it, as well as the safety of others.

 Digital Resources are available for this module at mentorbooks.ie/resources

We will explore:

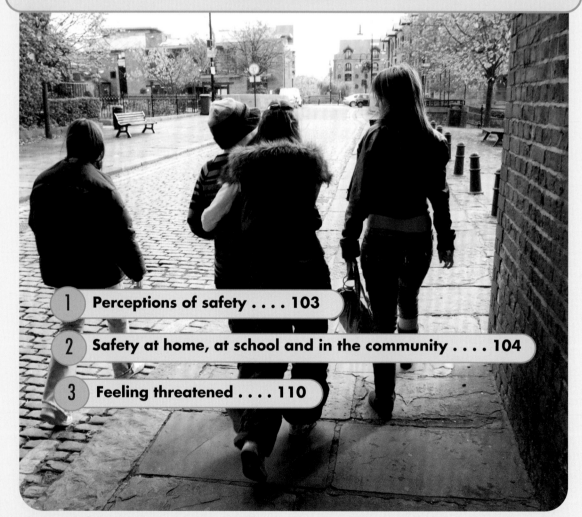

1. Perceptions of safety

Group ACTIVITY

1 **Brainstorm**

In groups, discuss any safety concerns you might have with the following day-to-day activities. Consider the level of risk for three of these activities and how you might make them safer.

(a) Bouncing on a trampoline

(b) Walking your pet Alsatian dog

(c) Walking to school

(d) Picking up an abandoned bag in a nearby field

(e) Babysitting toddlers

(f) Giving your contact details to an unfamiliar person on the Internet

(g) Giving directions to a stranger in a car

(h) Opening your locker during break time

(i) Crossing the road while texting

When you discussed the safety concerns in the activities above, you were actually performing a **risk assessment**. In your analysis you identified hazards, the level of risks for each hazard and you suggested measures to reduce the risk of harm to others. Employing measures to reduce risks is a way of taking responsibility for everyone's safety.

2. Safety at home, at school and in the community

1) **Safety at home**
Identify safety risks for each area listed below and the precautions you might take to avoid them.

(a) Bathroom
   Safety risk: _____
   Precaution: _____

(b) Kitchen
   Safety risk:: _____
   Precaution: _____

(c) Stairs
   Safety risk: _____
   Precaution: _____

(d) Windows and doors
   Safety risk: _____
   Precaution: _____

(e) Garden
   Safety risk: _____
   Precaution: _____

(f) Water wells
   Safety risk: _____
   Precaution: _____

(g) Street
   Safety risk: _____
   Precaution: _____

(h) Farm cattle shed
   Safety risk: _____
   Precaution: _____

(i) Farm machinery location
   Safety risk: _____
   Precaution: _____

(2) **Safety at school**

Review an average day at school and think about the school layout, furniture and student accessibility. In the table below identify the precautions taken in your school's safety programme.

Safety risk	How to avoid	Who is responsible?	Consequences

Schools are required to provide safe, secure and comfortable environments that enable young people to learn and share their concerns. Keeping students safe in school is every individual's responsibility so teachers and students must work together to make sure every person's safety is respected.

What you can do

● Get actively involved in making decisions that affect student lives: join the student council and health-promoting school teams. Go further with external agencies such as Comhairle na nÓg and other extra-curricular activities.

● Help fellow students through involvement in peer mentoring, buddy systems, anti-bullying and transition programmes.

If everybody takes part in creating a positive, caring and safe school environment, then there will be a greater sense of collective responsibility, pride and ownership.

All of us – parents, schools, communities and government – share responsibility to keep kids safe.

Bill Clinton

Safety in the community

Crossing the road safely

- Always stop and listen
- Be safe, be seen
- Eyes and ears on the road, not on your phone
- Find a safe place to cross

Cycling safety

- Always wear your helmet
- Check your bike has proper lights and reflectors
- Wear reflective clothing to be seen
- Obey all traffic signs, including traffic lights

NOTE

A recent survey by the Road Safety Authority revealved that Sunday is the most dangerous day of the week on Irish roads. The highest number of deaths (20) occur between 10 a.m. and 12 p.m., followed by between 4 p.m. and 6 p.m. (19).

Risky behaviour

Life involves taking some risks. A risk is when you partake in an activity that can result in loss, injury or death. We cannot see into the future, but by taking precautions we can reduce the likelihood of unwanted consequences. Some people are very prepared in their approach to taking risks: they learn as much as possible about the risk first. Some people take the risk without any thought for the consequences. Partaking in activities without using the necessary safety gear or paying attention to the safety guidelines is described as risky behaviour.

Wingsuit BASE jumping is a high-risk activity that involves participants jumping from fixed objects (Buildings, Antennas, Spans [bridges] and Earth [cliffs]) and using a parachute to break their fall. Advanced BASE jumpers have recently begun wearing wingsuits. These fabrics slow freefall rate and increase forward speed. The dangers of this particular sport are 50 times higher than conventional skydiving.

3 High-risk jobs

Below are some high-risk job environments. With your partner, name one job that is performed in each environment.

- At sea: _____
- On the road: _____
- In agriculture: _____
- At height: _____

WB3

Using the questions below, discuss the serious risks involved in these jobs.

(a) What type of person would be able to perform such high-risk jobs?

(b) What reason would they have for doing this type of job? Is it love or money?

(c) Do you think that a person could start in such jobs straight away?

(d) Do any of these jobs appeal to you?

Such dangerous jobs require people to be in harm's way every day. They are subjected to any number of dangers that vary according to the job in question. In all cases the workers are under environmental and emotional stressors to meet deadlines and quotas. Fatigue can also contribute to the risk involved. High-risk jobs can come at a high cost to the worker and their family.

4 Discussion

(a) Name three films that promote high-risk activity.

(b) Describe some of the risky behaviour that is featured in the films. How far-fetched do these films appear?

(c) What is the message about risk-taking that teenagers would receive from watching these films?

Paired
ACTIVITY

5 Taking risks

With your partner, discuss risks you think teenagers are likely to take. Then list five of these risks in the blank bubbles below. Some examples have already been filled in for you.

cheating in
an exam

getting
in a car
with a
stranger

telling
lies

cycling
with no
bicycle
helmet

behaving
violently

shoplifting

Your choice

Reviewing the consequences of risky behaviour in advance can help you decide the best option to take in a particular situation. Low- and high-risk situations can be examined in this way. Reviewing your opinion and the possible risks can help you become more assertive in your decision to ignore a bully or be the only person in your group of friends to say no.

6 **Examining the risk**

(a) In the table below rank the five risks you wrote about in the bubbles on page 108. You can rank each risk from 1 to 5, with 1 as the activity with the highest risk factor.

(b) Fill in the possible negative consequences of each risk and the precautions that could be taken to avoid them.

(c) Share your ideas with the class and write any further suggestions for precautions in the New column.

	Risk	Possible consequences	Precautions	New
1.				
2.				
3.				
4.				
5.				

TRB

3. Feeling threatened

ACTIVITY

WB3

1 **How would you feel?**
Examine the list of experiences in the table below. In the blank columns, describe how each experience would make you feel and what you would do in that situation.

How would you feel?	What would you do?	Experience
		(a) Walking down the road alone late at night
		(b) Being followed home
		(c) An adult shouting and pointing a finger in your face
		(d) A senior student taking your bag and passing it around to their friends to look through
		(e) Having your bag snatched by a thief on a bike
		(f) Receiving an email that threatens violence if you do not stay away from someone that the sender is attracted to
		(g) Catching a stranger staring at you in a cafe
		(h) Being pushed forward in the queue to get on your local bus
		(i) An older sister calling you stupid all the time

We don't always have the opportunity to consider in advance the consequences of taking a particular risk. We can find ourselves in risky situations over which we have less control, and so we may feel unable to cope with the threat to our safety.

ACTIVITY

2 **Threatening situations**

(a) Picture yourself in a threatening situation. How does your body react when you are feeling under threat?

_____

_____

(b) Why do you think our bodies react this way in threating situations?

_____

(c) Is feeling threatened a positive or negative experience? Explain how it makes you feel.

_____

Threats to personal safety

- Intimidation
- Attack
- Abuse

Strategies for self-protection

Intimidation

- Use the strategies for assertive communication in Module 3: Communication Skills, page 31.
- Practise saying 'No' out loud with conviction; make sure your body language is assertive to reinforce your message.
- Talk to an adult you trust if the intimidation or bullying persists. This is not a weakness on your part; some bullies need a firmer telling off before they see the seriousness of their behaviour.

> _He who runs away lives to fight another day._
>
> _Irish proverb._

Attack

Remember the 'fight or flight' response we have when we feel fear. When there is a chance to run away from an attack, it is advisable to take it!

- If a robber wants your money or possessions, then let him/her have them; this may reduce the chance that he or she will physically harm you.

- If you are being assaulted, scream as loud as you can for help; this could unnerve your attacker and give you the chance to run to the nearest safe place.

- At the start of any physical assault, it is best if you try to stay calm. Try not to fight back immediately, but think through any possibility for escape.

Abuse

- Abuse of any nature should be reported to the police or to somebody in authority.

- To abuse someone is to deny that person their right to be treated equally and with respect.

Asking for help

- In all of the cases concerning our physical health, our need to get help from others is obvious, whether it means saying 'No' to a friend or going to the police.

- There are many support groups and organisations set up to provide help in the various areas of personal safety. Some of these are listed in the useful contacts box on page 114.

Future Voices Ireland

'I received death threats, photo-shopped pictures of myself and constant torture. I felt so alone and had very few people I felt I could trust. It had become so bad and hurtful that I had to leave my school. It was one of the worst, if not the worst, experiences of my life.'

**Nathan McDonagh (17),
sharing his experience of threatening
behaviour online in *thejournal.ie***

Nathan is a member of Future Voices Ireland, a youth initiative which met with the president and head commissioner of the Law Reform Commission in 2015 to discuss the issue of cyber bullying in Ireland. The youth organisation presented a report detailing what they think needs to change in the way that we tackle cyber bullying. Future Voices Ireland believe it is 'extremely important that young people are at the heart of tackling this issue as it affects them in their everyday lives'.

The Commission is currently developing recommendations on cyber bullying legislation for Ireland.

(Read more at www.thejournal.ie, 'Cyberbullying victims speak out'.)

> **NOTE**
> Check out Future Voices Ireland at www.futurevoicesireland.org.

Group ACTIVITY

CSPE

3 Recommendations

(a) In small groups, decide on five recommendations you would make for cyber bullying (and related behaviour) legislation for Ireland.

(b) Compile a class list of recommendations and post them to the president and head commissioner of the Law Reform Commission.

This action could promote the belief in empowering young people in Ireland to get involved in policies that affect the younger generation.

Are you being threatened?

- If you received abusive or threatening messages or if someone is pressurising you to do something you don't want to do, it is never too late to get help.

- Don't give in to threats or send any replies. Walk away and tell an adult you trust or report to the contacts below. If you think you are in immediate danger call 999 or 112.

Useful contacts:
www.garda.ie
www.internetsafety.ie
www.childline.ie
www.webwise.ie
www.hotline.ie

End of Module Review

Class discussion

(a) Is there a particular help agency or support group that you think needs to be advertised in your school? Why?

(b) Organise a speaker from that particular agency or group to talk to your class to learn more about personal safety.

Notes

Notes

Notes

Notes

Notes

Notes